BATTLE OF CORINTH

The Lost Account of the

BATTLE OF CORINTH

and Court-Martial of

GEN. VAN DORN

By an Unknown Author

🔫 🔫 🔫

Introduction and Informal Essay
on the Battle
By
MONROE F. COCKRELL

🔫 🔫 🔫

BROADFOOT PUBLISHING COMPANY
Monographs, Sources and Reprints in Southern History
Wilmington, North Carolina

2003

BROADFOOT PUBLISHING COMPANY
1907 Buena Vista Circle
Wilmington, North Carolina 28405

THIS BOOK IS PRINTED ON ACID-FREE PAPER

ISBN 0-916107-32-9

EDITOR'S INTRODUCTION

In truth, the victory of the Union forces at Shiloh was not complete until the battle at Corinth, Mississippi, twenty miles distant and six months later.

The Federals had miraculously escaped defeat in the April battle on the Tennessee River. They had failed to follow up and clinch their victory. The Confederates with slight molestation had limped safely into Corinth to rest and prepare for another day. Here my story begins.

An unknown author, a man too modest to sign his name to his work, wrote and privately printed his account of this later battle calling it "Battle of Corinth," and signed it simply "By the Author." This inscription appears under a crude picture of himself. Diligent search failed to uncover his identity, and to my knowledge, only this one copy of his pamphlet has survived the years.

While writing my own story of this battle, I made several visits to Corinth. I interviewed many of the old citizens and other interested persons including the clear-minded Mrs. Eugenia Polk Hyneman, who assisted in preparing General Johnston's body for burial after Shiloh. I dug out old county and township maps, went over old roads and bypaths and followed the worn down breastworks of both armies, signs of which survive to this day.

But the finding of the old pamphlet was worth all my time and expense involved. E. J. East, the foremost historian at Corinth, now living in California, gave me my first account of it. He remembered having seen the little book many years ago at a farmhouse near Corinth. But, alas, he had forgotten the owner's name and location.

Many months went by before that family was found. They had all but forgotten the "Battle of Corinth" pamphlet—but were willing to search.

We rummaged through the old attic, in trunks and dresser drawers. No wonder it was difficult! The pamphlet had been sewed into an old ragged almanac. It was yellow with age and crumbling—but it was there!

It is a simple, straightforward recital. Its language is typical of the schools of those days. It tells the story just about the way an old-timer sitting around the Court House at Corinth would sum up what happened.

In my own account I have tried to put the battle in its relation to the War in the West with the addition of a few observations found in diaries, the Official Records, and all other reports of the battle that my search of years could lay hands on. However, I did not find any account that excels that of this unknown author in completeness, accuracy of statement and dramatic clarity. The Court-martial of General Earl Van Dorn sums up the weakness of the Confederate command and strategy, and adds mightily to the interest in the pamphlet.

My great uncle, General Francis Marion Cockrell of the Second Missouri Infantry, served under Van Dorn at Corinth. Years later, Col. Oscar L. Jackson of the 63rd Ohio asked him, "What drove you Confederates out of town?" Cockrell, remembering the bloody fight at Fort Robinette, replied, "Nothing drove us out. I watched the charge against your part of the line and when I saw you stay where you were, I knew the town was no place for us and we got out of our own accord."

I have turned over to Seale Johnson of Jackson, Tennessee, the pamphlet, my own map and other material. Now, after so many years, "Battle of Corinth" is being republished which I am happy to share with students and devotees of the War.

Monroe F. Cockrell

GENERAL VAN DORN

For his part in the battle, General Van Dorn was accused of many things—
that he was without proper map of the area, that he refused the services of
available artillery, that he went into battle without proper food for his men,
that he needlessly delayed attack, that he permitted the enemy to run
reinforcement trains, that he was guilty of cruel treatment of officers and
men. He was exonerated of all charges at the court of inquiry, yet to him
must be given the blame for a stunning Confederate defeat.

COL. W. P. ROGERS
Courtesy of Mrs. L. B. Outlar
September 1946

COL. W. P. RODGERS*

Just as Col. Rodgers reached Fort Robinette and climbed to its top, a strong reinforcement of Federals from their left wing appeared in sight. A glance at his small band of followers must have convinced the brave Colonel that further resistance was hopeless. Upon positive testimony of living witnesses, it can be stated that he made an effort to surrender by waving a white handkerchief from the point of a ramrod handed him by a soldier, but this effort was either disregarded or unobserved by the approaching troops, who fired a volley that brought down nearly all the brave men including the heroic Rodgers.

—from the Lost Account

*The unknown author used a "d" in the spelling of the Colonel's name throughout his account. The spelling was confirmed as Rogers by his daughter in 1946.

—M.F.C.

CORINTH, MISSISSIPPI

After the defeat at Shiloh, General Beauregard retreated to Corinth, where soon the Confederate forces numbered about eight thousand. Beauregard was unwilling to risk another battle and soon retreated to Tupelo. On Generals Van Dorn and Sterling Price fell the responsibility of reclaiming victory but they were not equal to the task.

FEDERAL SOLDIERS AFTER THE BATTLE

This picture shows the diversity of troops and kind of men fighting at Corinth. At the left is the mound where the guns of Battery Robinette cut down the brave troops of Van Dorn and Price, charging across the railroad tracks in their vain assault.

THE ASSAULT THAT FAILED

This is Robinette the day after the battle. Directly before us is a dead Confederate soldier who had swept along in his charge against the ramparts of Battery Robinette only to fall within fifty yards of the goal. To the extreme left of the picture is where the body of Colonel Rogers has been recently laid. The brave Texan leaped from his dying horse, and on foot dashed up the parapet straight into the last charge of grape-shot.

His dead battle-charger lies close to the rampart bearing witness to Rogers' courage and audacity.

BEFORE THE SOD HID THEM

The Confederate dead piled before Fort Robinette at Corinth on the morning after the battle. At the left lies Colonel Rogers and resting upon him is the body of the gallant Colonel Ross. This picture was taken by Armsted and White who were operating a studio at Corinth.

United Daughters of the Confederacy

To Erect a Monument to Colonel William P. Rogers.

The Texas division of the United Daughter of the Confederacy is raising funds to erect a monument to Colonel William P. Rogers, who led the Confederates against the Seventeenth Wisconsin Regiment of McArthur's brigade in the battle of Corinth, bravely meeting death during the charge.

Colonel Rogers lies at rest in Corinth, where the Union soldiers buried him after the battle, though there is no monument erected to his memory, which fact seems incredible to General John Crane, who was then adjutant of the Wisconsin Regiment, as will be noted from the following letter which was received by Mrs. A. R. Howard, president of the Texas division:

New York, N. Y., Nov. 27, 1906.—Dear Madam: In my recent interview with you at Governors Island I spoke to you of Colonel Rogers of Texas and promised to send you an account of his death.

The battle of Corinth occurred on October 3 and 4, 1862. General Rozencranz commanded our forces and Generals Price and Van Dorn commanded the Confederates. On the 3d we got the worst of it, and were forced into the Union breastworks, but early on the 4th the real battle began by a fierce assault on our lines, which for a time threatened to carry everything. The Seventeenth Wisconsin Regiment of McArthur's Brigade, of which I was adjutant, was placed in a position to defend Fort Robinette, which was occupied by a regular battery.

We had cut down several acres of timber in our front, forming an abatis as we felled the trees, so that all the tops pointed toward the foe. The limbs were trimmed and sharpened. It made a very formidable obstruction.

After an artillery duel in the early morning there was a lull, the Confederates no doubt getting their assaulting columns in position, and we were waiting for them.

Suddenly we saw a magnificent brigade emerge from the timber into the open in our front. They were formed in two lines of battle. The sun glistened on their bayonets as they came forward at right shoulder shift in perfect order—a grand but terrible sight. At their head in front of the center rode the commander, a man of fine physique, in the prime of life, quiet and cool as though he were taking his brigade on a drill.

Up to this time there was no firing on either side, when suddenly our artillery opened, the infantry followed and pandemonium reigned. The Confederates were tearing their way through the fallen timbers and notwithstanding the slaughter were getting closer and closer. Their commander seemed to bear a charmed life. Still on horseback, he was ordering, commanding and urging his men—going straight for Fort Robinette, and before he had realized it he had jumped his horse across the ditch in front of the guns and was in the midst of us. There he was shot dead, with some of his soldiers who got through with him. Then we learned who it was—Colonel William P. Rogers of the Second Texas, commanding a Texas brigade. When he fell the battle in our front was over. His brigade disappeared. How many escaped of the gallant brigade we never knew, but the slaughter was terrible.

We laid the body of Colonel Rogers reverently in the shade and covered his face with an overcoat. When the battle was over General Rozencranz came over and asked us to uncover his face. He said: He was one of the bravest men that ever led a charge. Bury him with military honors and mark his grave so that his friends may claim him. The time will come when there will be a monument here to commemorate his bravery."

This we did, and a few years ago I made a pilgrimage to Corinth and found the grave still there, marked as we had marked it, but there is no monument.

Surely this is wrong. The great state of Texas is full of men who love heroism and who are generous enough to see that a monument is erected to Colonel Rogers, worthy of him and worthy of the state. With best wishes, I remain, yours sincerely,

(Signed)   John Crane.

By courtesy of Mrs. L. B. Outlar, Wharton, Texas, a daughter of Mrs. M. R. Bolton, and a granddaughter of Col. Wm. P. Rogers. His monument at Corinth was unveiled Aug. 15, 1912.

Monroe F. Cockrell
3-12-1946

THEY PHOTOGRAPHED THE AFTERMATH OF THE BATTLE

The Author.

CONTENTS

Comprehensive Map by Mr. Cockrell follows page 83

THE LOST ACCOUNT

DEDICATION

To

THOSE HEROES WHO FELL

AT

CORINTH, DAVIS' BRIDGE AND TUSCUMBIA

AS WELL AS

THEIR SURVIVING COMRADES-IN-ARMS,

WHO

STILL LINGER ON THIS SIDE OF THE RIVER,

THIS VOLUME

IS RESPECTIVELY DEDICATED

JANUARY, 1899   BY THE AUTHOR

THE UNKNOWN AUTHOR'S PREFACE

This unpretentious story has been carefully compiled from data obtained from different sources. In addition to official records, the writer has interviewed a score or two of old soldiers who participated in the battles around Corinth. Not less than fifty letters have also been received, with information of more or less importance. Some of these letters were from officers of high rank, others from privates. Great care has been taken to be accurate in all statements made. It is believed that many facts herein stated have never before appeared in print. At the same time it is not claimed that the work is clear of errors. No human work is, but if this shall add aught to the true history of the bloody drama it attempts to describe, it will abundantly satisfy.

THE AUTHOR.

BATTLE OF CORINTH

OCTOBER 3rd AND 4th, 1862

*Including also the Battles of Hatchie Bridge
and Tuscumbia Bridge, October 5, 1862*

THE EXPEDITION which resulted in the Battle of Corinth was planned and commanded by Gen. Earl Van Dorn, of the Confederate army.

About the 1st of August, 1862, he broached the project of a combined attack to Gen. Sterling Price, who commanded two divisions of infantry and a brigade of cavalry on the M. & O. Railroad. Several letters passed between these officers and an agreement was finally reached on the very day that Price fought the bloody but indecisive battle of Iuka. When Price's troops returned from Iuka to Baldwyn they remained at the latter place only until Sept. 26th when they resumed their march to Ripley, the county seat of Tippah county, a strategic point affording a good base from which to maneuver and assail Corinth. Gen. Van Dorn had one division of infantry and two or three regiments of cavalry at or near Holly Springs. These troops were set in motion for Ripley which place they reached only a short time before Price.

Both commands reached Ripley on the 28th. Here they remained over a day to rest.

Generals Van Dorn and Price met, discussed and agreed

17

upon the details of the proposed expedition. The plan formulated by Gen. Van Dorn was substantially as follows:

To march from Ripley to Pocahontas on the M. & C. Railroad, threaten Bolivar, Tenn., where there were 8,000 Federal troops under command of Gen. Hurlbut, then turn suddenly and march against Corinth, storming the strong entrenchments before the Federal forces could be concentrated for defense. Gen. W. S. Rosencrans commanded the Federal garrison at Corinth. He was a brave and skillful officer, but it was thought possible to attack him before the troops from Rienzi, Burnsville and other outposts[1] could be brought in. There were 15,000 Federals in Corinth and about 10,000 at the outposts mentioned.

Field returns at Ripley showed that Van Dorn had 20,000[2] men of all arms. The only hope of Confederate success lay in attacking before the enemy could concentrate.

Nearly all the Confederate troops were veterans. There were only a few regiments who had not received their "baptism of fire." Among those who had never participated in a general engagement may be mentioned the 35th and 43rd Mississippi of Moore's brigade, both destined to win honor in the approaching conflict. Other regiments had already won imperishable renown, among them may be mentioned 1st, 2nd, 3rd, 4th, 5th and 6th, Mo., the 1st, 2nd, 3rd, 6th and 9th Texas; the 3rd La.; 14th, 16th, 17th, 18th, 19th, 20th and 21st Ark. Some of these brave troops had participated in the sanguinary battle of Wilson's Creek, Mo.; others in that of Pea Ridge, Ark.; and still others in bloody Shiloh and the fierce conflict at

---

All footnotes indicated by numerals are explanations made by the Editor. Those with asterisks are by the author and from the original edition.
[1] Iuka, Jacinto and Bethel, Tenn.
[2] 22,000

Iuka, besides many other battles and skirmishes, in all of which they had displayed the highest qualities of soldiership.

In Lovell's division were to be found the immortal 15th Mississippi, whose valor at Fishing Creek and Shiloh had never been excelled; also the 6th Mississippi whose loss of 70 per cent at Shiloh sufficiently attested the bravery of its men. The 22nd Mississippi was another splendid regiment, nor should the 37th Alabama, the 3rd and 7th Kentucky or the 9th Arkansas be forgotten. All these had won laurels on hard fought fields. It is not intimated that the foregoing constituted all the veteran troops of the Confederate army, or that a single regiment was unreliable or doubtful in the face of the enemy.

The consolidation of the commands of Van Dorn and Price had an inspiriting effect on the troops of both. They now felt that that they were in sufficient force to make effective headway against the enemy.

On the afternoon of Sept. 28th, Gen. Van Dorn issued an order at Ripley directing that three days rations be cooked. This order recited further that all empty wagons be' at once dispatched to Holly Springs for additional food supplies, and closed by directing that on the afternoon of the next day, (29th), Gen. Lovell should move his division 5 or 6 miles north on the Ruckersville road, this being also the road to Pocahontas.

Soldiers in the camp at Ripley were kept busy for the next few hours preparing rations, burnishing arms and making other preparations for the expedition, which all felt would be one fraught with important results.

Gen. Lovell's division moved out promptly at the time ordered and took the Ruckersville road, camping near the Luker place on one of the branches of Muddy, preceded by a detachment of cavalry.

Next morning, (30th), the two divisions of Gen. Price broke camp and followed. The whole army was now in motion toward Pocahontas. The main body of the Confederates encamped at the village of Jonesboro, 16 miles north of Ripley, Lovell's division still in the lead, its advance reaching Metamora, 2½ miles from Pocahontas, which place, a station on the M. & C. Railroad and 40[3] miles west of Corinth, was reached and occupied by these troops early on the morning of Oct. 1.

The village of Metamora occupied a high ridge overlooking the valley of Big Hatchie. Here the State Line road, running from Middleton to Corinth, crossed the Ripley-Pocahontas road at right angles and descending the steep incline, westward[4] toward Corinth, crossed Hatchie river at Davis' Bridge and climbed the rugged timber-clad heights beyond. Over this State Line road must the Confederate army pass in its march to Corinth, but first it was necessary to repair the bridge at Davis' Mill which had been partially destroyed by the enemy, and a detail from Lovell's division was assigned to this work.

The necessary repairs were so far completed that Lovell's division crossed during the afternoon[5] and camped along the State Line road on the east side of Hatchie, Gen. Price's troops remaining on the west side.

Early on the morning of Oct. 2 Gen. Lovell's troops, Rust's brigade in front, took up their line of march toward Corinth, a detachment of Armstrong's cavalry brigade acting as the advance guard. A portion of Gen. Price's command was also moving at an early hour, crossing Hatchie before daylight.

Gen. Wirt Adams was left on the west side of Hatchie

---

[3] 20 miles, Pocahontas to Chewalla 10—to Corinth 10 miles.
[4] Eastward
[5] October 1st

with about 700 cavalry, consisting principally of his old regiment, to guard the roads in the direction of Middleton and Bolivar, to report the presence and dispute vigorously the advance of the Federal force stationed at the latter place upon the Confederate rear. Especially was his command to guard the bridge over Hatchie. About two miles from and east of Hatchie a road known as the "Boneyard Road" joins the State Line road, coming from a southwestern direction, nearly parallel to the river. Where these roads join, Gen. Van Dorn left the Confederate wagon train and with it, as a guard, the 1st Texas Legion under command of Col. Hawkins, with instructions to move his regiment and two reserve batteries left with him to the assistance of Gen. Adams, should it be necessary in order to defend the bridge.

About four miles east of the point where the wagon train was parked the road[6] to Corinth crosses the Tuscumbia, a small sluggish but miry little river, that flows from the southeast and empties in the Hatchie[7] just below Pocahontas. The Tuscumbia was spanned by a wooden structure called "Young's Bridge," because of a man of that name whose residence crowned the hill near by, on the east side. This bridge had been partially destroyed by the Federals and they had left a small cavalry picket to dispute the passage of the stream. These pickets fled in confusion, after exchanging a few shots with the Confederate advance, with a loss of one killed and two wounded. This was the first blood shed on the expedition.

Here another halt was necessary while awaiting repairs on the bridge. The Confederates were stretched along the road for miles. It was ideal October weather, though rather warm. Many of the soldiers employed the time of the stop in gathering muscadines, which were quite plentiful in the swamp. In a few

6 State Line
7 Wrong: N of RR and NE of "P"

hours the bridge was repaired and the advance begun. There was light skirmishing with the front of Rust's brigade and the enemy between the Tuscumbia bridge and Chewalla but not sufficient to check the advance. Chewalla, a station on the M. & C. Railroad was reached before night, and the enemy's camp containing a few tents and commissary supplies was captured. Here Gen. Rust halted his brigade and awaited the remainder of the command which reached that point during the evening and encamped for the night, throwing out a strong picket. Gen. Van Dorn also dispatched a regiment of cavalry to cut the M. & O. Railroad about six miles north of Corinth.

Here for a moment we will leave the Confederates and see what was transpiring in the Federal camp. Gen. Rosencrans had been at first doubtful as to the objective point of the expedition, but on the morning of October 1st he became satisfied that Corinth was the point to be attacked. He then sent couriers with dispatches to all outposts to hurry the concentration of all the troops at Corinth. It is evident that Gen. Rosencrans had an exaggerated idea of the Confederate strength—something, by the way, common with most Federal writers who have written about this battle. There were four full divisions of Federal troops at and near Corinth, to-wit: Hamilton's, Stanley's, McKean's and Davies, besides some cavalry. At daylight on Oct. 3rd, three of these divisions were marched out west from Corinth, to a position near the outer intrenchments, and took position as follows: Hamilton on the right, east of the M. & O. Railroad, Davies in the center between the two railroads while McKean was on the Federal left, with three regiments advanced to the outer works occupying both sides of the M. & C. Railroad. Stanley was kept in reserve in the southern part of Corinth.

We will now return to the Confederate camp at Chewalla. Before the dawn of day the troops were astir and were soon in motion toward Corinth. Gen. Villepigue's brigade of Lovell's division, consisting of the 33d and 39th Mississippi regiments and Dupiere's battalion of Zouaves, was in front. These troops encountered the Federal pickets about 5 miles from Corinth who fell back with but slight resistance for two miles, when Cane Creek was reached, a small stream crossed by the railroad at right angle. The bridge over this stream had been torn up by the enemy and had to be repaired before the artillery could be brought over. This work was done under a sharp fire from the enemy's skirmishers. When completed the division crossed. As it was now manifest that the Federals were in front in force, Lovell's division was placed in line of battle, south of the railroad,[8] in the following order:[9] Villepigue's brigade on the right with cavalry flankers, Bowen's in the center and Rust's on the left, with left flank resting on the railroad. Near the same time Price's corps was deployed on the north side of the railroad as follows: Moore's brigade, with its right resting on the railroad, formed Price's right. Phifer's brigade on Moore's left with Martin's brigade on Phifer's left, then Cabell's brigade in reserve; then Gate's Missouri brigade on the left then Green's brigade with cavalry flankers, with Colbert's brigade in reserve.

The alignment of troops was completed about 10 o'clock.[10] Skirmishers were thrown forward and the Confederate line at once began to press steadily in the direction of the enemy. A commanding hill occupied the front of Lovell's division, south of the railroad and a short distance west of Boone's Crossing, its summit crowned with artillery supported by a strong force

---

[8] M & C Railroad
[9] Villepigue on left, Rust in center-reserve, Bowen on right.
[10] A.M. October 3rd

of infantry. The west side was honey-combed with rifle pits, filled with sharpshooters. It was necessary to carry this strong position by assault. The skirmish line was strongly reinforced during a temporary halt and the assault was ordered. Emerging from the dense woods the gallant troops of the charging columns raised the *rebel yell* and made a dash for summit. An open space of about 200 yards lay in front which must be crossed before reaching the base of the hill. This ground was covered by fallen forest trees and swept by artillery and small arms at close range, and the Confederate loss was heavy, but their onward course was not checked for a single moment by the carnival of death. Across the plain and up steep hillside they rushed, scattering and capturing the sharpshooters, then on to the summit from which the Federal troops fled precipitately. Two regiments, the 9th Arkansas and 22d Miss., reached the summit almost simultaneously, followed closely by the 3d and 7th Ky., Carothers' (Miss.), Battalion, the 1st. Mo. and 33d Miss. The Federals were subjected to a heavy rear fire as they fled down the east side and sought another position, leaving a splendid 24 pound Parrot gun, the "Lady Richardson," together with a caisson, in the hands of the victors.

The battle had been short, sharp and, for the time, decisive. The losses were heavy on both sides. The Federals retreated to an intrenched camp about half a mile rearward. Lovell's division was halted. The troops had shown superb fighting capacity but their part in the great battle was now practically over. Their conduct in the face of the enemy proves conclusively that no blame can be imputed to them for failure to participate actively in the subsequent events of the bloody drama.

We must now turn our attention to Gen. Price's column on the north side of the railroad, the advance of which had commenced at about the same time that Lovell's men had moved against the enemy. Moore's brigade, on Price's extreme right, first came under fire. Crossing a corn field, Moore's men were temporarily halted on the east side. A strong skirmish line, consisting of two companies of the 2d Texas, under Major Timmins, and two, (F. and K.), of the 35th Miss., under Capt. R. H. Shotwell, were sent forward.*

T HESE SKIRMISHERS advanced thro' the woods a short distance until they became involved with those of the enemy and a lively exchange of shots began. This skirmish continued some time without important results when an advance of the whole line was ordered. The line of battle advanced rapidly, sweeping back the enemy's skirmishers who took refuge behind the outer intrenchments[11] where the bulk of the Federal army was lying in line of battle.

Advancing steadily through the fallen timber which covered the ground some distance in front, the Confederates speedily drove the Federals from the works, capturing a number of prisoners, and pursuing closely the discomfited and retreating foe. In this pursuit of the enemy, Moore's brigade soon passed the left of Lovell's division where it had halted immediately after capturing the fortified hill, and moving rapidly on came to a point opposite the intrenched camp to which the federals had fled when driven from the hill by Lovell's men. Reinforced by two Arkansas regiments, Moore crossed[12] to assault the camp. The Federals had rallied, were

---

*Maj. Shotwell is now a respected citizen of St. Louis and the writer is indebted to him for valuable information about the battle. Speaking of this skirmish line, he says: "We advanced some 300 yards through woodland and undergrowth, down to a narrow ravine and after crossing the same continued to advance up a gently ascending slope covered with small bushes, not seeing a foe but realizing that each step brought us nearer to a concealed line of Federal infantry. None save those who have experienced it can appreciate the suspense of such moments."
11 Old Confederate
12 To South side of M & C RR

heavily reinforced and met the attack with firmness and valor. Formed in double line, the front line kneeling and the rear line firing over their heads, they poured a withering fire into Moore's rapidly advancing troops. But nothing could check long the advance of the victorious Confederates. Recoiling for a moment, they soon rallied, rushed forward with resistless enthusiasm, capturing the camp, a number of prisoners, quartermaster's and sutler's stores, the Federals escaping with their artillery.

This closed the fighting for that day with Moore's brigade, except some skirmishing as the troops having recrossed to the north side of the railroad, advanced toward Corinth.

During this time the remainder Price's corps had been heavily engaged and equally successful. The brigades of Phifer, Green, Martin and Gates advanced promptly. The 1st. Ark., (sharpshooters), under Col. E. L. Stirman* formed the skirmish line and engaged the enemy promptly and boldly, notwithstanding a heavy fire of grape and canister, driving the Federals rapidly back upon their first line of light works. Reinforced by the main line of battle, the Confederates swept the enemy from these defenses in gallant style. The brave Col. Martin, commanding 4th brigade, fell in this conflict, and the command devolved on Col. McLane, of the 37th Miss. Lieut. Col. Leigh, of the 43d Miss., was also slain, together with many other brave men. The enemy's loss was heavy in killed, wounded and prisoners. Two pieces of artillery were captured. The federals fled behind their second line at the "White

---

*Col. Stirman, who now resides in Denver, Col., in a valued communication to the writer, says: "In the very midst of the fight a splendid bay horse came running into our lines, riderless. I sent him to Gen. Maury's quartermaster that evening, and the next day, after storming the works, having my horse killed in the charge, Gen. Maury hearing of the fact sent me this horse to take the place of mine. This horse I kept and rode through many an engagement during the war, taking him home with me to Fayetteville, Ark., after the war closed."

House," about one mile from Corinth. As soon as the proper dispositions could be made, this position was attacked by the Confederates with great energy and determination and the Federals were again forced back with heavy loss.

This was a fierce engagement and lasted an hour, beginning about 4 p.m.

The Federals retired in a demoralized condition behind their last line of works. The Confederates advanced to the heights overlooking the town, which they hoped would soon be in their possession.

It was now about 6 p.m. and the sun was setting. In front of Price were Forts Robinette and Powell, while south of the M. & C. Railroad and in front of Lovell's division were two strong positions known as Battery Williams and Battery Phillips.

Fort Robinette, about 200 yards north of the M. & C. Railroad, was flanked on the south by a formidable line of earthworks extending to the railroad, with a deep ditch in front. On the north a line of earthworks connected it with two strong bastions on slightly higher ground than than that occupied by the main fort, and distant from it about 200 to 300 yards respectively. These bastions were furnished with strong batteries. Fort Robinette, thus strongly flanked and bristling with heavy guns, manned by regular artillerists with strong supports, was indeed the strongest part of the line and well nigh impregnable.

Fort Powell occupied an eminence on the east side of the M. & O. Railroad and was also a strong position.

Behind this cordon of strong defenses the flying Federals, defeated in all the engagements of Friday, had taken refuge and reinforced by the reserves they awaited the Confederate assault. It cannot be denied that both Federal officers and men were, at this time, exceedingly apprehensive of the results of immediate attack. Preparations looking to a probable retreat had been made as soon as it was ascertained that the tide of battle was going against them, and these were now redoubled.

But the attack was not made.

Gen. Price said his troops were too much fatigued, too hungry and thirsty to risk a final attack at this late hour. In this opinion Gen. Van Dorn was induced to concur, some say reluctantly.

THERE IS NO QUESTION that the men were really much exhausted; especially were they suffering from thirst. The region over which they had passed during the day's fighting was and is one devoid of springs and running streams, except during the rainy seasons. No rain of consequence had fallen in several weeks and the troops had no opportunity to secure water beyond the limited amount obtained from a few scattering wells. The day had been quite warm for October and the heat had aggravated their thirst. These facts are stated in order to show that there existed grounds for the decision reached by the Confederate commanders. What would have been the result of a sweeping charge on Friday evening can only be a matter of conjecture. Many officers and men, who participated in the battle, do not hesitate to say that it would have been successful. No one can doubt that had Stonewall Jackson or Forrest been in command the assault would have been made.

During the night the Confederates had but little to eat, and with difficulty supplied themselves with drinking water, drawn from wells in the deserted Federal camp and elsewhere.

The commanders on both sides were busy during the night, making preparations for the morrow's conflict, which both realized would be bloody and decisive. Trains were heard rumbling and whistling, cheered upon their arrival by the Federals in Corinth. This has led many to believe that the Federal army was heavily reinforced during the night, but there is no proof that such was the fact. The great benefit to the Federals was the time given them in which to change positions of two divisions. McKean's division had borne the brunt of the day's conflict and was considerably demoralized thereby. This was withdrawn from Fort Robinette and outlying defenses and its place filled by Stanley's splendid division of fresh troops.

Gen. Van Dorn also made some changes during the night. Lovell's division was left on the south side of the M. & C. railroad, Maury's division in front of Fort Robinette; Hebert's division was on Maury's left, parallel to the M. & O. railroad, with its left almost touching the railroad.

The batteries of Maury's division were placed on a high hill, 600 yards west of Fort Robinette,[13] with orders to open a heavey fire upon the enemy's works about an hour before daylight. Hebert's division was then to advance against the Federal right wing, pivoting on its own right, and swinging across and down the M. & O. railroad, attacking the enemy with vigor.

As soon as the roar from Hebert's attack should be heard, Maury's division was to advance to the assault, moving straight to the front toward Corinth. Lovell's division was then to assault Fort Phillips and Williams, on the south side of the M. & C. railroad.

It was midnight before all these dispositions were made and the two armies sank to rest for a brief period before beginning the bloody work of the next day.

About 4 a.m. the three batteries of Maury's division opened, almost at the same instant, a terrific fire from their

---

[13] South of M & C RR

elevated position fronting Fort Robinette, which was kept up until daylight.

When it ceased the expected advance of Hebert's division on the left did not take place. Gen. Van Dorn dispatched a staff officer with all possible speed to ascertain the cause of delay. He failed to find Gen. Hebert. Two others were sent with similar result. Finally Gen. Hebert reported at headquarters, sick, and asked to be relieved from command that day. This was 7 o'clock. Much valuable time had already been lost, and more was necessarily lost by Gen. Green, who succeeded Hebert in command of the division, before he could acquaint himself with the position of the different brigades sufficiently well to direct the movements of the troops intelligently.

In the meantime, about 9 o'clock,[14] the skirmishers in front of Gen. Maury's line became engaged with those of the enemy. This skirmish grew hot, especially in front of Moore's and Phifer's brigades, and about 10 o'clock an advance was ordered on this part of the line.* This movement drew a tremendous artillery fire, yet the Confederates, during the first part of the advance, were so protected by timber that their loss was small. But when they emerged from this shelter and entered the open space in front of the intrenchments, and distant not over two hundred yards in front of Fort Robinette, the loss of life was appalling. Leading up to the main fort was only one narrow, open way, the remainder of the ground being covered by abattis and other obstructions that made progress exceedingly difficult. Over these obstructions the brave troops of Mississippi, Texas, Arkansas and Alabama made their way under a withering, desolating fire from front and right flank, of both

---

[14] Brig. Gen. John C. Moore

*"Phifer's brigade was formed as follows: 6th Texas on right, joining Moore's left, then 3d Ark., 2d and 9th Texas with Stirman's sharpshooters on the left"—R. H. Deadman, Princeton, Ark.

artillery and small arms, the like of which was seldom experienced, even in the bloody civil war. It took heroic souls to face this avalanche of destruction and they were there. Every moment lessened their numbers, but the sight of falling comrades did not for an instant cause the survivors to waver or falter. *With a fixed determination and sublime disregard of danger and death, the uneven line of Confederates pushed forward to the intrenchments and drove the Federals from all that part of the line north of Fort Robinette, including that strong fortress itself.

The 2nd Texas, a portion of the 35th Mississippi the 6th and 9th Texas and one company of the 42nd Alabama came immediately in front of the Fort. Owing to the greater obstructions in front of Robinette, as well as the more concentrated and deadly fire encountered, when this handful of dauntless men, led by Col. W. P. Rodgers, of the second Texas, reached the Fort the remainder of the brigade and division, to the left and north had already pressed the Federals from the works and were in swift pursuit toward town.

J UST AS COL. RODGERS reached the fort and climbed to its top, a strong reinforcement of Federals from their left wing appeared in sight. A glance at his small band of followers must have convinced the brave Colonel that further conflict was hopeless. Upon the positive testimony of living witnesses it can be stated that he made an effort to surrender by waving a white handkerchief from the point of a ramrod, handed him by a soldier, but this effort was either disregarded or unobserved by the approaching troops, who fired a volley that brought down

---

*"Col. Sol. Ross, of the 61st Texas of Phifer's brigade was mounted on a beautiful snow white mare. In climbing over the trees she, in some way got away from the Colonel and went flying out about the time we reached the works or just before, causing many to think that the gallant rider had been slain and it was so reported."—Col. Stirman

nearly all the brave men who stood near including the heroic Rodgers.

While this memorable and tragic scene was being enacted at Fort Robinette, the remainder of Moore's and Phifer's* brigades of Maury's division, and Gates' and Green's brigade's (the latter commanded by Col. Moore. of 43rd Mississippi), of Hebert's now Green's division, were sweeping on into Corinth.

The two brigades last-named were all Missourians except one regiment and a battalion of Mississipians. In their impetuous advance these men had come upon Fort Powell, a strong fortification on an elevation, just west[15] of the M. & O. railroad and north of town, which they captured after a desperate struggle together with 20 pieces of artillery. McLane's and Colbert's brigades were on the extreme left in this charge. But few men of these two brigades reached Fort Powell, but run against Hamilton's division of Federals, to the west of the Fort, and retired after a short conflict.

Meantime the troops who had captured Fort Powell were pressed by the rallied Federals and were nearly out of ammunition. Cabell's Arkansas brigade was ordered to their support by Gen. Green. The Arkansians hurried to obey orders. The distance was considerable, and before they could reach Fort Powell the Missourians had been compelled to relinquish it to the enemy and fall back. In falling back it happened that they took a different road to the one upon which the Arkansas troops were advancing to their support, so when Cabell's men arrived before the fort they were astonished to find it occupied by the Federals. But like brave men, as they were, they raised a shout

---

*"Gen. Phifer was a brave officer. Well do I remember his passing me after I was wounded, hat in hand, cheering on his men to victory or death."—H. C. Dial, Sulphur Springs, Texas.

[15] East is correct.

of "Butler" and gallantly charged the Fort. *The 20th Arkansas regiment went over the works together with the 21st and Jones' Battalion, the latter suffering very heavy loss, but were unable to capture and hold the place against Hamilton's entire division, which was now massed against them, and were forced to fall back. The 18th and 19th Arkansas and Rapley's Battalion of sharpshooters were to the right of the Fort and followed Maury's division and a portion of Green's brigade into Corinth.

Into the very heart of the town rushed the Confederates, driving the Federals before them from house to house. They soon reached and passed Rosencrans' headquarters, which were at the house now occupied as a residence by Mr. Fred Elgin. Onward they swept to the Tishomingo House at the railroad crossing. Near this point the brave Col. Moore,[16] of the 43rd Mississippi, commanding Green's brigade, fell pierced by a bullet and mortally wounded. The Confederates had by this time become badly scattered and were in no condition to meet the attack made upon them by Sullivan's fresh brigade of Federal troops, which had been held in reserve in the western part of town and which Gen. Rosencrans now hurled against them.

Broken and disordered the Confederates could make no effective resistance to this attack and began to fall back, slowly and stubbornly, firing backward as they retired, notwithstanding the heavy artillery cross fire to which they were subjected from the batteries at Forts Robinette and Williams. There was no chance to rally these men under the circumstances, but it is certainly remarkable that no panic was observed among them. Back, back, they retired, passing slowly over the grounds cov-

---

*Senator Berry, of Arkansas, then a lieutenant, lost a leg in this part of the field while bravely leading his company to the assault.
16 W. H. Moore

ered by their charge and entered the woods northwest of
Corinth on their retreat.[17]

Lovell's division had made no assault on their part of the
line. Why they did not is a question to this day. The failure
was not the fault of the troops, for they were men who had
never failed to do their full duty. Gen. Lovell's official report
says the entire forenoon was consumed in getting into proper
position that he was just ready to order an advance when he
received word that Price's corps was defeated and retreating,
and that his division must cover their retreat.

Villepigue's brigade was accordingly marched out and
formed across the line of retreat. Through their ranks passed
the retreating troops, weary and downcast, plodding slowly to
the rear. No wonder Gen. Price shed tears when he viewed
the thinned ranks of his fire corps and noted the sullen and
disheartened appearance of the survivors.

That the Federal army was badly stunned by the heavy
blows it had received is amply proved by the failure to pursue
except in a feeble way. The regiment of cavalry that was sent
in pursuit was unsupported by infantry, and was easily driven
back by a few charges of grape and canister from one of
Villepigue's batteries. The battle was over in two hours and
the Confederate army in full retreat before 1 p.m. This retreat
was not molested further than has been mentioned and the
army reached Chewalla by nightfall where it was halted for
the night.

Here Gen. Van Dorn ordered Col. W. S. Barry, of the
35th Mississippi to take a detachment and go back under a
flag of truce to bury the Confederate dead. Permission to do
this was, however, refused by Gen. Rosencrans, who said that
he would have this duty performed by his own men, which he

---

[17] 2 P.M.

did but in a very hurried and imperfect manner, if we are to believe citizens who witnessed the interment.

At Chewalla a courier brought a dispatch to Gen. Van Dorn from Gen. Wirt Adams, who, it will be remembered, was left to guard Davis' Bridge, on Hatchie river. The dispatch stated that the Federal force from Bolivar had already reached a point within two or three miles of the bridge. This force consisted of two brigades and two extra regiments of infantry and one regiment of cavalry—in all about 9,000 men—and was commanded by Gen. Hurlbut. Hurlbut's command had left Bolivar early on the morning of the 4th, coming by the way of Middleton where it struck the State Line road leading directly to Davis' Bridge.

A few miles east of Middleton the Federals encountered Wirt Adams' cavalry, but the latter made but a feeble effort and never checked the advance for a moment. The Confederates were driven back rapidly across Big Muddy without being given time to burn the bridge behind them, and were followed by the Federal cavalry and Lauman's brigade of infantry to the east side of Big Muddy, where the Federal infantry halted and bivouacked for the night. The Federal cavalry made a feint as though to go the bridge that night, but were persuaded to believe that the force in front was too strong.

IT IS NECESSARY NOW to recall the fact that the Confederate wagon train had been parked about two miles east of the Hatchie, where the Boneyard road intersected the State Line road, and that the 1st Texas Legion, commanded by Col. Hawkins, and two batteries of artillery had been left as a guard and, if necessary, to join in defense of Davis' Bridge. Gen. Van Dorn dispatched a courier to Col. Hawkins to move out his regiment promptly to the defense of the bridge, together with the batteries. This dispatch reached Col. Hawkins at 7:30 on the morning of the 5th, and in a few minutes the Texans were rapidly moving toward the Hatchie, 360 strong, which they reached at 8:30, and were immediately deployed in line of battle on the east side of the bridge, under orders from Gen. Adams who here met them.

The Federals had begun their advance at an early hour. Veatch's brigade, which had crossed Muddy before daylight, was put in advance. They met with no resistance until they reached the Robinson place, about one mile[18] from Matamora. Here they encountered Adams' cavalry pickets, in a barn, who were driven out by a few shots from a battery and the advance, scarcely checked, was resumed, the front of their column reaching the village and heights of Matamora very nearly at the same time that Hawkins' Texans reached the bridge. The federals immediately began forming their line of battle along the heights, planting one battery in Sam Carper's yard, in the fork of the roads, and another to the right, on another eminence, both commanding the valley in front.[19]

Before these batteries had been placed in position by the Federals, Gen. Adams, for some unexplained reason, ordered Col. Hawkins to cross the Hatchie with his regiment and, dividing it into two equal parts, place his men in line of battle on the west side of the bridge[20] and on both sides of the road. By this time Gen. Maury had reached the bridge and took command, ordering Dawson's battery to take a position about 150 yards west of Davis' house. About this time the remnants of Maury's division began to arrive, having been hurried forward by orders from Gen. Van Dorn to assist in holding the bridge,

---

18 West
19 To the East.
20 Davis

as the loss of the position meant the probable destruction of the entire Confederate army.

Gen. Moore's brigade was in front and the 35th Mississippi in front of the brigade, which did not now number over 500 men rank and file.

As Moore's men passed over they filed to the right, down the Hatchie, and formed in line of battle parallel to the stream. However, before all had gotten across the Federal batteries at Matamora opened so hot a fire on the bridge and its approaches that a portion of the 2nd Texas, in the rear of the brigade, was unable to cross and remained on the east side. As soon as possible the left of Moore's brigade was connected with Hawkins' right and the entire command advanced to a small branch, known as the Burr Branch, where they halted in a strip of woods, about four hundred yards[21] from the Hatchie. Dawson's battery had in the meantime been gallantly answering the enemy's heavy artillery fire and suffered the loss of nearly all its horses.

Ceasing fire of artillery, the Federal battle line began now, about 12 m., to advance, the Federals shielding themselves as much as possible by the fences, ditches and hedges which intervened. The Confederates opened a withering fire of small arms upon the advancing Federals and charged, driving them back some distance, only to be charged in turn and driven back to the position they first held. During this conflict a regiment of Federal infantry had quietly moved to the right of Moore's brigade, taking position in a cornfield within musket shot, without being observed by the Confederates. From this position they poured a volley in the Confederate right flank, and began immediately to advance with the evident intention of placing themselves between the Confederate line and the

---

21 West

river. It was necessary to retreat in order to avoid destruction. Hawkins' regiment being nearest the bridge all succeeded in crossing thereon, as did a portion of Moore's brigade, but the most of the latter were cut off from the bridge by the rapid advance of the Federal right, and were cooped up in a bend of the river, where most of them—some 200 or 300—were captured, the balance escaping across as best they could, some on a drift and others by swimming, though nearly all lost their arms. All but one piece of Dawson's battery was captured by reason of the horses being killed.

On the east side[22] reinforcements had arrived. First Phifer's, then Cabell's brigade had reached the place and been put in position on the hillside fronting the Hatchie, with batteries posted so as to cover the bridge. Thus far the battle had been a Federal victory, but the tide was now to turn.

GEN. ORD HAD ARRIVED EARLY in the morning and assumed command of the Federal forces. Flushed with success, he now decided to make the same fatal error that the Confederates had made in the morning—cross Hatchie and attack. It can be urged, in Ord's behalf, that he thought the Confederates too badly demoralized to offer effectual resistance, but in this opinion he overlooked the fact that it was practically a new command that he was confronting. In pursuance of Gen. Ord's plan of battle, the Federal infantry was massed and a dash made for the bridge. Here ensued a scene of carnage with few parallels. Ask any living Federal soldier, who participated in this charge, where he encountered the heaviest fire of the war and he will answer, without hesitation, "Hatchie Bridge." The Confederate batteries were admirably posted within easy range,

---

22 Of the Hatchie

while the hillside was covered with Phifer's Texans with rifles trained on the bridge and its approaches.

As the blue column moved forward with platoon front, at a double quick, it was met with a terrific storm of shot, shell and minnie bullets. The front ranks melted down and clogged the way, but the survivors pressed on till the bridge was reached. Here the storm redoubled its fury, piling the narrow bridge with dead and wounded, many of whom fell into the water beneath. But in spite of terrible loss, the Federals pushed across and secured lodgment on the east side of the river. Gen. Ord himself was severely wounded on the bridge and the command reverted to Gen. Hurlbut. Several desperate assaults were made on the hill in front, but each time the Federals were repulsed with great slaughter.*

Had the Confederates at this time made a determined assault, the whole Federal command would probably have been captured or dispersed. No such attack was made, however, the Confederates contenting themselves with holding their position, skirmishing with the enemy until 3:30 P.M. and then slowly withdrew. The Federals were too badly crippled to pursue. The Confederates fell back and took their line of march up the Boneyard road towards Crum's Mill, six miles above Davis' Bridge. Here was a bridge which had been repaired by two companies of the 7th Tenn. cavalry, over which the wagon trains and artillery passed, followed by the troops, except Bowen's brigade, which had been left to guard the rear at Tuscumbia bridge, and continued their retreat toward Ripley.

---

*Our men would lie down and could not be seen until the enemy were within 75 yards of our line. We would allow them to approach until we could see the whites of their eyes, then without exposing ourselves in the least we would pour volley after volley into them, cutting them down like grass. No men on earth could stand such a fire. Our men were all fine shots and nearly every shot must have taken effect. I never saw such slaughter in my life. They fell by the hundred, then recoiled, reformed and rushed to meet the same result. It was impossible to drive us from the position by direct attack.—Col. E. L. Stirman

We now return to Corinth. Rosencrans, as we have seen, was slow to pursue the retreating Confederates. No effort was made in this direction until the morning of the 5th, when two brigades of fresh troops, under Gen. McPherson, were started in pursuit, followed soon after by the remainder of the Federal army in two divisions on parallel roads. Through some mistake these columns became entangled with each other on the march, and were thereby much delayed, the main body not reaching Chewalla until nightfall.

McPherson's command, however, was not delayed and marched past Chewalla about p.m., reaching the vicinity of Tuscumbia bridge about an hour before sunset, when he struck the pickets of Bowen's brigade of Confederates. Deploying, he pressed these pickets back upon the Confederate line of battle, formed on the east side of the bridge. The heaviest demonstration was against Bowen's center, which was held by the heroic 15th Mississippi. Gen. Bowen took command of this regiment in person and advanced them about 15 paces, when they poured such a deliberate and well aimed fire into the Federal ranks that the latter retired precipitately and did not renew the attack in force. There was light skirmishing until dark, when Bowen withdrew his brigade, destroyed the bridge as much as possible, and retreated south during the night.

The Confederate army passed through Ripley and continued to retreat to Holly Springs. The Federals pursued as far as Ripley and then abandoned the pursuit.

The Federals report their loss at Corinth at 315 killed, 1812 wounded and 232 missing. There is no data to hand as to their loss at Tuscumbia bridge. Gen. Bowen reported his loss there to be 3 killed and 12 wounded, and the Federal loss is known to have been heavier.

Detailed report of Confederate losses at Corinth will be

found in appendix. Also a partial list of Confederate losses at Davis' Bridge. The Federals report finding 32 Confederate dead on this battlefield. The Federal loss at Davis' Bridge was heavy. They admit a loss of 50 killed, 493 wounded and 17 missing.

THE COURT-MARTIAL OF
GEN. VAN DORN

Court of Inquiry

Following is a synopsis of proceedings of court of inquiry, held upon the suggestion of Gen. Bowen, of Mo.

The court was constituted as follows: Gen. Price, Gen. Lloyd Tilghman, Gen. D. H. Maury and Capt. E. H. Cummings.

Maj. Wright was advocate for Gen. Van Dorn.

The Following specifications of charges against Van Dorn were filed by Gen. Bowen.

1. That he was unprovided with map of Corinth and surrounding country.

2. Refusing services of artillery officer and not reconnoitering.

3. Going into battle without proper food supplies.

4. Delayed attack on Friday evening.

5. Allowing the enemy to run trains and reinforce on Friday night.

6. Cruel and improper treatment of officers and men.

Gen. Rust, (first witness.)—Did not know whether Van Dorn had a map or not. Had plenty of food supplies. Told Gen. Lovell at the Tuscumbia, en-route to Corinth, that the attack was bound to fail. Thought that Van Dorn would try to maneuver the enemy out of Corinth. Attack should have

43

been pressed on Friday evening. X. Had a little skirmish before reaching Chewalla, Oct. 2. Camped his brigade in advance that night. Moon was shining brightly on the night of the 3d, and the men were eager to advance. Lovell's command was in good condition if Price's was equally so an attack would have been expedient. Thought attacks by night, by troops not veterans, extremely hazardous and only to be made under extraordinary circumstances. Such circumstances, in his opinion, existed at the close of the first day's battle.

Gen Bowen.—The party sent on Oct. 2 to repair bridge across Tuscumbia found a Yankee picket, skirmished with them and wounded three. On march from bridge to Chewalla, Lovell's men were constantly driving the enemy's skirmishers. March from Chewalla to Corinth, 10 miles, was tedious and tiresome, owing to frequent deploying into line, skirmishing etc. Did not think Van Dorn intended direct attack on the works at Corinth; thought he intended to maneuver enemy outside and then attack. Did not believe it absolutely necessary to make a night attack on the 3d Oct. Attack would have been finished by 8 p.m. Saw the Federal center was broken and retreating before a line of Confederate skirmishers. He believed that a charge made by Lovell's division at that time would have driven the enemy; pell mell, from the town.

Gen. Green.—Did not think the Federals were evacuating Corinth on night of the 3d, as many did. The reason was that he could hear the chopping of timber inside the enemy's lines and twice, when trains came in, he heard loud cheering. Never saw Van Dorn drunk.

Gen. Price.—Knew Van Dorn had a splendid map of Corinth and its defenses. Gave it to him. It was captured at battle of Iuka. Thought that the successes on the 3d should be followed up promptly, but was uncertain as to whether Lovell was ready or not. Talked with Gen. Van Dorn that night about the noises to be heard in Corinth. Did not think he heard the noises himself. Never had seen Van Dorn drunk. Had known him since a few days before the battle of Elkhorn, March 1st, 1862.

Gen. Maury.—Did not think the advantages gained on the 3d should have been further pressed. Did not think Van Dorn could have prevented the enemy from reinforcing that night. Could not tell by noises whether the Yankees were reinforcing or evacuating. It was impossible to make a reconnoisance of the Federal fortifications that night, as pickets were not over 100 yards apart. Felt sure Van Dorn was not unduly addicted to the use of liquor. Never saw him drunk. X. Gen. Moore took his brigade right into the main part of town, capturing a battery of light artillery where they crossed the M. & O. Railroad, taking possession of the Tishomingo Hotel and depot buildings. Part of his brigade including 2d Texas under Col. Rodgers, entered Ft. Robinette, where Rodgers was killed. Phifer's and Cabell's brigades entered town on Moore's left. Had known Van Dorn since 1846, when American army entered Monterey, during the Mexican war. Thought him incapable of cruelty and injustice.

Capt. Tobin.—Was commanding battery in Maury's division and was captured by enemy on road between Fts. Williams and Robinette, before daylight on morning of Oct. 4. Was carried back into Corinth as a prisoner. Saw Gen. Maury's division drive the Federals over the high bridge on the M. & C. Railroad and clear out of the town. The Confederates followed as far as the Tishomingo and Corinth Hotels. Was sure the Federals expected total defeat, because they sent wagon and ordnance trains to the rear and he was ordered to report at Hamburg, on the Tennessee River.

Col. J. T. Ward.—Had known Van Dorn since he commanded military posts in Texas and Indian Territory, in 1857. Saw him almost daily from 1857 to 1861. Never saw him take but two drinks and never saw him drunk.

Lt. Col. Major.—Was with Van Dorn at the battle of Elkorn and since, Had always considered him a very temperate man.

After considering all the testimony, of which the foregoing is only a brief excerpt, the court of inquiry acquitted Gen. Van Dorn of all the charges preferred against him. Gen. Bowen, who preferred these charges, lived less than a year after, dying[23] soon after the capture of Vicksburg, from disease contracted during that memorable siege.

---

[23] In fact, Bowen died on the night of July 13, 1863, after his parole that very day.

LIST OF TROOPS PARTICIPATING IN THE BATTLE
OF CORINTH

Following is a complete roster of Confederate forces engaged in the Battle of Corinth.

MOORE'S BRIGADE.

35th Miss. Infantry.
42d Ala. "
15th Ark. "
23d Ark. "
2d Texas "
Bledsoe's Battery.

CABELL'S BRIGADE

18th Ark. Infantry,
19th Ark. Infantry,
20th Ark. Infantry,
21st. Ark. Infantry,
Jones' (Ark.) Battalion Infantry
Rapley's (Ark.),
Sharpshooters.

PHIFER'S BRIGADE

6th Tex. Dismounted Cavalry,
9th Tex. Dismounted Cavalry,
3d Ark. Dismounted Cavalry,
1st. Ark., (Stirman's Sharps'rs,)
McNally's Battery

GATES' BRIGADE.

1st. Mo. Dismounted Cavalry,
2d Missouri Infantry,
3d Missouri Infantry,
5th Missouri Infantry,
16th Ark. Infantry,
Wade's Battery.

GREEN'S BRIGADE.

43d Miss. Infantry
4th Mo. "
6th Mo. "
3d Mo. Dismounted Cavalry.
7th Miss. Bat. Inf.
Guibor's Battery,
Landis' Bat'y.

*MARTIN'S BRIGADE.

37th Ala. Infantry,
36th Miss. "
37th Miss. "
38th Miss. "
Lucas' Battery.

*Gen. Martin was killed in first day's battle; brigade commanded in second day's battle by Col. McLane of 37th Miss.

48 *THE LOST ACCOUNT*

COLBERT'S BRIGADE.
40th Miss. Infantry,
*1st. Texas Legion,
3d Tex. Reg't.,
14 & 17th Ark. Inf.,
consolidat'd
3d Louisiana Infantry.
St. Louis Battery,
Clark's Bat'y.

JACKSON'S CAVALRY.
1st Miss. Cavalry, (Adams.)
1st Miss. Cavalry Partisan
Rangers
2d Miss. Cavalry
2d Ark. Cavalry (Slemmons.)
2d Mo. Cavalry
(McCullough)
7th Tenn. Cavalry
Unattached Companies.

BOWEN'S BRIGADE.
1st. Mo. Infantry,
15th Miss. "
6th Miss. "
22d Miss. "
Carothers' Miss. Bat. Inf.
Watson's Battery.

RUST'S BRIGADE.
31st. Ala. Infantry,
35th Ala. "
4th Ala. Infantry Battalion.
9th Ky Infantry,
3d " "
7th " "
Hudson's Battery.

VILLEPIGUE'S BRIGADE.
33d Miss. Infantry,
39th Miss. "
Dupeire's Battalion Zouaves.

*Left near Hatchie Bridge to guard wagon train.

CONFEDERATE LOSSES.

HEBERT'S DIVISION.
Gates' Brigade.

	K	W	M
1st Mo. Cavalry,	9	54	15
2nd Mo. Infantry,	19	122	21
3rd Mo. Infantry,	5	65	23
5th Mo. Infantry,	6	62	19
16th Ark. Infantry,	13	29	12
Wade's Battery,	1	0	2
Total,	53	332	92

Second Brigade (Colbert's.)

3d La. Infantry,	0	12	20
3d Texas Cavalry,	2	29	13
1st Texas Legion,	3	17	75
14th Ark. Reg't.	0	12	2
17th Ark. Reg't.	1	13	6
40th Miss. Reg't.	5	46	16
St. Louis Battery and Clark's Battery,	0	0	0
Total,	11	129	132

Third Brigade (Green's.)

4th Mo. Infantry,	15	87	27
6th Mo. Infantry,	31	130	53
3rd Mo. Cavalry,	12	62	26
7th Miss. Battalion,	6	23	36
43rd Miss. Infantry,	13	56	156

	K	W	M
Landis' Battery,	0	6	4
Guibor's Battery,	0	5	0
Total,	77	369	302

Fourth Brigade (M'Lain's.)

	K	W	M
Staff of Brigade,	1	1	0
36th Miss. Inf.	12	71	0
37th Miss. Inf.	19	62	0
38th Miss. Inf.	4	31	0
37th Alabama,	5	35	0
——— Battery,	0	3	0
Total,	41	203	0

RECAPITULATION

	K	W	M
First Brigade,	53	334	92
2nd Brigade	11	129	132
3rd Brigade	77	369	302
4th Brigade	41	203	0
Total Hebert's Div.	182	1033	526

MAURY'S DIVISION.

Moore's Brigade.

	K	W	M
42nd Ala.	0	17	352
Lyle's (Ark.) Regt.	5	23	116
35th Miss. Regt.	32	110	347
2nd Texas Regt.	10	34	122
Bledsoe's Battery,	0	1	1
Boone's Ark. Reg't.	6	51	68
Total,	53	230	1002

SKETCH OF COL. W. P. ROGERS[24]
Written by His Daughter

The following sketch of Col. Rogers, 2d Texas, was prepared by his daughter, Mrs. M. R. Bolton, of Wharton, Texas.

Col. W. P. Rogers was a native Georgian.

He was born Dec. 27, 1817. His parents moved to Mississippi when he was a child, and his babyhood and early manhood were spent in that state.

He graduated at a medical college when quite young, but as that was not his chosen profession, he commenced the study of law on reaching his majority.

In 1840 he was married to Miss Martha Holbert, and during his life she was a true and loving helpmate.

Col. Rogers fought with distinction in the Mexican war, commanding a company in Col. Jeff Davis' regiment of Mississippians. The dashing A. K. McClung was Lieutenant Colonel of this regiment. He was the first man who scaled the walls of Monterey and Capt. Rodgers was the second.

During President Taylor's administration Capt. Rogers was sent as consul to Vera Cruz, Mexico. He filled that office for two years with honor and then resigned and moved to Texas. He settled in Washington, Washington county, where his brilliant talents soon placed him first in the legal profession. His reputation as a criminal lawyer extended over the state, and his services were sought far and wide. He never prosecuted in a murder case, but was generally successful in the defense.

---

[24] Spelling "Rogers" confirmed by Mrs. L. B. Outlan March 8, 1946.

Col. Rogers was not a rabid secessionist. He deplored, but felt the necessity of secession. He was an intimate friend of Gen. Sam Houston, and though differing with him politically, perhaps understood and appreciated the position that grand old man took in his firm adherence to the Union better than almost any other man.

Having moved to Houston in 1859, Col. Rogers was sent as a delegate from Harris county to the secession convention, and signed the secession ordinance.

He was offered the command of a regiment in Virginia, but at the solicitation of his wife accepted, instead, the position of Lieutenant Colonel of the 2d Texas infantry.

The following spring the 2d Texas was sent east of the Mississippi river. Col. Rogers was detained by sickness, but joined his regiment just on the eve of the great battle of Shiloh, and was welcomed with the greatest enthusiasm by that gallant band. In this battle he was distinguished for bravery, and promoted to Colonel on the field. The regiment was only a few skirmishes after this until the battle of Corinth.

Col. Rogers' courage and his heroic death on Corinth's bloodstained field are matters of history. He led in the assault on Fort Robinette and with scores of his brave men falling around him, yielded up his noble life, under his colors, which he had planted upon the enemy's stronghold.

His deeds of heroism won the admiration and reverence of both armies, "the blue and the gray," and a generous foe gave him a military burial with the honors of a general.

Col. Rogers left to his children the legacy of an unsullied name, and a fame that will live while a Southern heart throbs with love for, and pride in, this sunny Southland of ours.

BATTLE OF CORINTH

By

MONROE F. COCKRELL

An informal study of a great battle first delivered as an address at Lake Forest Academy, Lake Forest, Illinois, March 8, 1946.

FOREWORD

F OR years I have been interested in knowing what caused Grant, after missing the battle at Iuka, to disappear from nearby Burnsville, Mississippi. There, as commander, he had issued orders directing the Federal forces to unite against Price at Iuka.

Grant's usual practice was to move toward an impending battle rather than stand immobile in its vicinity, as on this occasion. I believe I have found the answer in the paper of General D. S. Stanley, U. S. A., on "The Battle of Corinth" read on December 4, 1895 before the New York Commandery of the Loyal Legion and printed in their Second Series, 1897, Page 271.

General Stanley said: "The failure of communication between Grant's (forces under Ord) and Rosecrans' forces was very unfortunate . . . . Our Union hopes were disappointed, and a general quarrel arose between Generals Grant and Rosecrans that had far-reaching, and I believe, very sad results. This occurred in the middle of September. Price retreated to Tupelo. General Grant returned to Jackson, Tennessee, where he fixed his headquarters, and Rosecrans retained his camp about Corinth."

This long buried record of dissension in the high command throws new light on Federal activities at Iuka, the battle at Corinth and their barren pursuit. It gives a clue to the long sought answer to the question, "Why wasn't Grant present at the Battle of Corinth?"

M. F. C.

December 24, 1954

54

T HE FEDERALS under Grant had a miraculous escape from defeat at Shiloh on April 6, 1862. At the close of the second day, the Federals with heavy reenforcements, were victorious, and the Confederates, under Beauregard, retreated to Corinth. They were back in their old trenches on April 9th. Grant had had enough—only feeble efforts were belatedly made to follow up the costly victory.

Shortly after Shiloh, Halleck arrived and took charge. He had big plans—he wanted more men, more guns, more food, more everything, and his Government could and did meet his requests. While assembling all this, Halleck reorganized his army with Grant second in command—no duties.

It was not until April 29th, three weeks after the battle of Shiloh, that Halleck was ready to move. On that day, he started his army, now swollen to about 110,000 men, by several roads to Corinth. That army was well fed, well rested, abundantly equipped and bigger than any force ever assembled in the Mississippi Valley. Halleck had begun the most historic crawl in military history—it took him 30 days to travel less than twenty miles.

By night of May 1st, he occupied Monterey where he camped. He had made ten miles in three days. Between May 2nd and May 24th he alternately marched and intrenched.

On the 24th, he began building a fortified line about five miles long. It was called the "Halleck line."

It ran from the Mobile and Ohio Railroad on the northwest to and beyond Farmington on the southeast of Corinth. It was too long to be adequately defended and was abandoned right soon after Halleck was transferred to Washington in July.

On the night of May 28th, Halleck built intrenchments opposite the Confederate breastworks around Corinth—he was now close to a fight. In twenty-seven days he had moved up eight miles. On that tramp, he never saw enough Confederates to fill the Corinth calaboose. Even on the night of the 28th and the next day, nothing more than isolated skirmishes occurred.

FEDERAL OCCUPATION OF CORINTH, MAY 30TH.

By daylight on that morning Beauregard, completely deceiving Halleck and Grant, had retreated southward behind the Tuscumbia with his army of about 53,000 effectives.

The Federals immediately occupied the town. Now, they were in possession at the junction of two railroads—one that reached northward through Jackson, Tenn., to Cairo, Ill., and the other that extended westward ninety miles to Memphis, also on the river. Their supply lines were secure—everything could be brought in easily and quickly. Those 110,000 men would not have to live "off the country."

Halleck and Grant were satisfied—it was time to rest. Little attention was paid to the retreating Confederates although that first day in Corinth, Halleck must have known that Beauregard's army was less than half the size of his own. Nothing more than a late pursuit was undertaken and that petered out in about ten miles. Beauregard had escaped—it was Shiloh again. Nothing had been learned by that costly victory.

Let's turn back a moment. Hardly had Halleck and Grant found a place to sleep on May 30th, when Halleck did the most amazing thing—he broke up his army. An army that was fully prepared:

To follow up and destroy Beauregard;

To slide into Chattanooga and northern Alabama which were lightly defended at that time, or

To head straight for Vicksburg.

Halleck had everything but a courageous heart!

Anyway, June 1st, Halleck sent Buell back into Middle Tennessee and in July, Thomas' Division was also sent. Chattanooga was their objective along with repair of railroad lines that old Forrest had torn up. This work slowed up Buell.

July 11th, Halleck was transferred to Washington, but before leaving, he put Grant in charge.

In the meantime, the Confederates kept on southward fifty miles to Tupelo, where they stopped and awaited developments. On June 17th, Beauregard turned the army over to Bragg and took a sick leave. President Davis heard about it through Bragg and immediately seized the chance to appoint Bragg permanent commander on June 20th. The Confederates soon found out that Halleck was not going to bother them.

When Bragg learned or suspected that Buell was headed for Chattanooga, he planned to get there first and be ready to oppose him. If successful, he proposed to push boldly northward through Tennessee into Kentucky.

During the week ending August 5th, Bragg's army was on its way. August 28th, Bragg left Chattanooga heading for Kentucky, and Kirby Smith started from Knoxville two weeks earlier.

August 30th, Bragg put Van Dorn (near Holly Springs) and Price at Tupelo in charge of operations in West Tennessee. Immediately after Bragg's departure from Tupelo, Price

offered to cooperate with Van Dorn against Grant at Corinth
to prevent his reinforcing Buell.

August 11th, Bragg also ordered Van Dorn to cooperate
with Price. Nothing was done because Van Dorn's troops were
scattered. Breckinridge was over on the Mississippi between
Baton Rouge and Port Hudson and other troops were away
on outpost duty.

September 1st, while moving northward from Chattanooga, Bragg heard that Rosecrans (at Corinth) was about
to cross the Tennessee to cooperate with Buell, who was now
supposedly moving toward Nashville, Tenn., so Bragg ordered
Price (at Tupelo) to follow Rosecrans and prevent their
juncture.

September 4th, Price again suggested that Van Dorn
(near Holly Springs) unite with him, but Van Dorn, instead,
wanted troops from Price and wired that he could not move
for about ten days. Van Dorn was planning to move northward in West Tennessee towards Paducah or "wherever circumstances might dictate." Price replied that he could not
wait more than three days and would then start.

Fight at Iuka Sept. 19th

September 4th, to execute Bragg's orders, Price started
from Tupelo and occupied Iuka on the morning of the 14th.
There he was soon surprised to learn that Rosecrans had only
sent three divisions to join Buell, and that Rosecrans himself
with two divisions was near Jacinto, less than ten miles west
and a little south of Iuka.

Shortly after Sept. 4th, Van Dorn gathered his scattered
forces near Holly Springs and started northward to make a
demonstration in favor of Price's movement. He drove the
Federals out of Grand Junction and followed them to within

about seven miles of heavily fortified Bolivar where Hurlbut had plenty of men and siege guns. He was there by Sept. 20th.

When Price found out about Rosecrans and his lessened force, he quickly saw the chance to recapture Corinth, so he wired Van Dorn that he would unite with him against Corinth—the opportunity was simply too tempting for him. He was about to forget all about where he was going. I say "about" because hardly had Price wired Van Dorn when Price received another message from Bragg asking him to hurry across the Tennessee river to cooperate with him (Bragg). Now this was the very thing that Grant and Rosecrans feared would happen. Rosecrans sent a message to Grant that he had better watch the "old Woodpecker" lest he (Price) get away from them.

In the meantime, Van Dorn was doing some thinking about Corinth while moving northward to Grand Junction. On September 11th, President Davis yielded to his persuasions and placed Van Dorn in superior command—and this, supposedly, without consulting Bragg.

During the night of September 18th, one of Van Dorn's officers reached Iuka where he advised Price of Van Dorn's appointment and delivered his order for Price to unite with Van Dorn for an attack on Corinth. Price immediately began his preparations to leave. Alas! he did not know what was in store for him on the coming day.

As soon as Grant (at Burnsville) heard that Price was at Iuka, he started Ord from there to approach Iuka from the north and ordered Rosecrans to strike in from the west (Jacinto). By sundown on Sept. 18th, after moving leisurely, Ord stopped within a few miles of Iuka. On the next morning, he was to hold his fire until he heard Rosecrans' guns which was hardly expected before afternoon because of his longer march.

Price had nearly all of his infantry and artillery facing Ord while preparing to move. During the late afternoon of the 19th, his pickets on the Jacinto road were driven in by the advance troops of Rosecrans who were strung out along the road in loose marching order.

Price, instead of awaiting attack, promptly shifted a part of his force into line of battle across the Jacinto road together with a piece or two of artillery and gained the advantage in the earlier fighting. The Federals in the rear had failed to move up and spread out fast enough. Price had taken Rosecrans by surprise. A fierce struggle ensued and lasted for about an hour. Only a small part of the opposing forces were engaged when darkness ended the fighting. Ord and his men took no part.

The Confederate officers were badly shaken by the death of Gen. Henry Little. After his burial during the night, a consultation was held. All of Price's subordinates advised a retreat because of the obvious superiority of the Federals for the coming day. The decision was right because of Ord's presence to the north with an open railroad line behind him to bring in more troops from Corinth—a short twenty-two miles away.

By way of comment, the Confederates had about 14,000 and the Federals about 17,000. Only a small part were engaged, and each side lost about 700 men.

The next morning, Price and his army headed back towards Baldwyn.

Here again—now Grant was in supreme command—the Federals made only a feeble pursuit. The Confederates took nearly five days to march the thirty miles and were hardly molested.

Three times now within a distance of less than fifty miles, the Confederate army had been allowed to escape. There was Shiloh in April, Corinth in May, and now Iuka in September.

From Baldwyn on the 25th, Price advised Van Dorn of his setback and the consequent disruption of their plans. Van Dorn directed Price to unite with him at Ripley.

September 28th, both commands reached Ripley with the following troops. Price with the Army of the West in two divisions.

Maury's Division
        J. C. Moore's Brigade
        Cabell's   "
        Phifer's   "
        Armstrong's Cavalry
        Gates' 1st Brigade
        Colbert's 2nd   "

Herbert's Division
        Gates'   1st Brigade
        Colbert's 2nd "
        Green's   3rd "
        Martin's 4th "   14,000

Van Dorn with Lovell's Div. of Dist. of Miss.
        Rust 1st Brigade
        Villepigue 2nd Brigade
        Bowen 3rd Brigade
        Jackson's Cavalry   8,000

Van Dorn's own report, dated Oct. 20th, gives the background of his reasoning that, to him, justified his attack upon Corinth, regardless of Price's losses at Iuka, and regardless of support that Bragg wanted sent into Middle Tennessee to insure success of his march into Kentucky.

Although Corinth was the strongest, it was the most salient point. Its capture was a condition precedent to the accomplishment of anything of importance in West Tennessee.

A sudden attack there, before outposts could be called in, would soon lead to the fall of Bolivar and Jackson. In the event of Bragg's failure in Kentucky, the whole valley of the Mississippi would be lost before winter.

Memphis would afford no advantage in expelling the Federals from West Tennessee. To attack Bolivar would bring help by rail from Jackson, and both flanks of the Confederates would be open.

T HE CONFEDERATE plan was to move north from Ripley to Metamora, some twenty-eight miles, threaten Hurlbut at Bolivar, and then suddenly turn on the 15,000 Federals in Corinth before their troops could be called in from their outlying posts.

The plan had risks aplenty:

It involved a march of fifty miles in hot, dry weather along a narrow broken road, densely wooded all the way. There was no water after leaving the Hatchie until they reached Corinth and vicinity. The first thirty miles could be taken in stride, but the last twenty from Metamora to Corinth, required accelerated speed every single mile, and a sudden headlong attack with accurate timing at the very end of the fifty miles. Surprise and secrecy were first essentials right up to the town. Furthermore, failure at Corinth meant an immediate demoralizing retreat along the same road—in other words, ten days of heavy marching with most of the time taken up in hard fighting.

Nevertheless, Lovell's Division moved out of Ripley on the afternoon of September 29th, and Price with two divisions followed the next morning.

The entire command was at Chewalla, Tenn., by the night of October 2nd, but the Federals had been warned some ten miles out from Corinth. There was skirmishing all the way between the Tuscumbia and Chewalla.

The element of secrecy was out. The Federal troops were soon called in from the outposts at Burnsville, Iuka, Jacinto, Rienzi and Danville, each about twenty miles from Corinth.

The next morning, Oct. 3rd, the march was resumed with Lovell's Division again in the lead. Near Alexander's house, a short five miles from Corinth, the Federal infantry picket line was driven back across Cane Creek. Here a halt was necessary to repair the bridge.

Notice that this was an infantry picket line—where was the Federal cavalry? It was on patrol duty on every front except this road—the main direct one from Chewalla to Corinth.

By the time the bridge was repaired, the Confederates found out that the Federal army was behind the old Confederate line of intrenchments. After crossing Cane Creek, they moved into line of battle facing their old line some three quarters of a mile away and along a rolling ridge. It was now about ten o'clock in the morning and the Confederates were only about three and one-half miles from town.

It was not until noon when the Confederates were ready. Then they stormed up the ridge. In front of Price was a quarter mile of felled timber, and in front of Lovell was a hill that swarmed with men and Federal artillery. This hill also had rifle pits on the west side and was also protected by 200 to 300 yards of felled timber.

The Confederate lines never faltered, but their losses were very heavy and inevitable.

The Federal divisions under Hamilton and Davies, with a part of McKean's, were forced and flanked backward. They made five different stands.

1st Outer line—old Confederate breastworks.

2nd—about 1,000 yards back of the Outer Line.

3rd—about 800 yards further back at junction of Columbus and Chewalla roads.

4th—about 950 yards further back at what is the "White House Line."

5th—about 725 yards still further back upon Robinette, which was about 675 yards from the railroad crossing in Corinth.

It was now between four and five o'clock. The Federals were behind their "Inner Line" and the Confederates were fagged out. Since daylight, they had travelled ten miles with heavy fighting more than half the way. They halted to rest— scattering fire was heard and then came darkness. The first day was over—the Confederates were in front of Corinth, but night gave the Federals time to bring in the troops from the outposts many of whom were already approaching the town.

The court martial of Van Dorn (Nov. 1862) brought out the idea that if two more hours of daylight had been given them, the Confederates would have carried and held the Federal works, but General Price qualified this by adding to his testimony "with the cordial support of Lovell." Gen. Bowen testified that Lovell appeared to be undecided and seemed to be awaiting orders. Lovell was separated by the M. and C. Railroad and the dense woods with the consequent loss of close contact.

BATTLE OF CORINTH OCT. 4TH

During the night of the 3rd, both sides rearranged their lines. The Confederates planned their attack from three directions. From the north and east of the Mobile and Ohio Railroad. From the north between the M. and O. on their left and the Memphis and Charleston Railroad on their right. From the west with their left on the M. and C. R. R.

On the morning of the 4th, before dawn—about 4 a.m.—the Confederates opened a heavy artillery fire directly from the north and west against the town and the Federal "Inner Line." There was a spirited reply.

Gen. Buford, of Hamilton's Division, wrote, "It was grand. The different calibers, metals, shapes and distances of the guns caused the sounds to resemble the chimes of Old Rome when all her bells rang out."

After daylight, there was a long lull in the artillery fire, but skirmishers were moving in and out of the dense woods feeling for strong or weak places in the opposing lines. There was desultory firing by Confederate sharpshooters who were more than annoying.

Between 9 and 10 a.m., the Confederates began forming their columns—deep columns—in the edges of the woods and here and there in plain sight. Col. Jackson wrote in his diary, "All the firing ceased and everything was silent as the grave."

THE DRIVE AGAINST HAMILTON ON THE RIGHT
OF BATTERY POWELL

About 10 a.m., the main attack started. It had been delayed while Green was taking charge after Hebert had reported being sick. Two Confederate columns (Martin's and Colbert's Brigades of Hebert's Div.) moved en 'echelon eastward across the M. and O. R. R. and the Purdy road about one-half mile north of Battery Powell to attack Hamilton's right wing.

Three times these columns drove against the right wing on Hamilton's north front. Although they made temporary dents in parts of his line, they were always thrown back and had to retire after about an hour's fighting.

But other brigades of Hebert's Division (Gates and W. H. Moore) had a shorter route and better success. Their attack struck Hamilton's left, and their heavy columns, debauching from the woods along Purdy road and along the east side of the M. and O. R. R., literally ran over his troops and batteries, projected to the north of Battery Powell, driving everything back helter-skelter along and behind Davies' Division. The Federals rallied on Davies' reserves and then, in turn, flung back the Confederates, recaptured Battery Powell and the high ground around it. The Confederate Gen. Cabell was sent in support but enfilading fire from Battery Williams played havoc with him so he never got up until after the Confederate retreat had started. There was nothing for him to do but join it.

THE DRIVE AGAINST DAVIES ON THE LEFT
OF BATTERY POWELL

Following their orders, the brigades of Maury's Division (J. C. Moore and Phifer) delayed their attack until they heard the firing on their left.

Phifer's brigade and a part of Moore's swept down from the north, along the west side of the M. and O. R. R. through the dense underbrush, vines and fallen timber of Elam Creek flat, and broke out into the open at the M. and O. R. R. and the gap in the Federal light works near the left end of Davies' line. Here near the railroad, they drove through the Federal right center.

Some say Davies' line broke at the first fire thereby causing the break-through by Gates and W. H. Moore at Battery Powell. "In fact, our troops on the right gave way rather easy" wrote Col. Jackson in his diary. Others under Davies say that everything was going well when all of a sudden the artillery-men deserted their guns at Battery Powell and then the supporting infantry gave way in confusion.

In any event, all agree that the Confederates pierced the Federal lines in both places, and some of W. H. Moore's men fought their way clear down close to the depot—all the way from Battery Powell.

The left wing of J. C. Moore's brigade (heretofore mentioned), ahead of Phifer, struck the extreme left end of Davies' line, somewhat to the right of Phifer's thrust and joined in driving through the Federal right center under Davies.

The fierceness of the assaults by the brigades of Phifer and John C. Moore carried them into the streets of the town.

The fighting swept from one house to another, and the Confederates drove the Federals out of the houses by firing through the windows.

It was then about 11:30 a.m. Their impetuous rush had carried them across vacant lots, around houses and down Jackson street past the headquarters of Rosecrans, past Halleck's and on down to the Tishomingo Hotel and the buildings around the depot at the railroad crossing.

Other Confederate troops swept further eastward down around the Corinth House at Filmore and Foote streets.

The official records of the Federal commanders bestow fulsome praise upon their men for checking the onslaught of the Confederates east of the M. and O. R. R. and for hastening their retreat.

But there is one bit of testimony that might interest you. I refer to "The Colonel's Diary" by Col. Oscar L. Jackson of the 63rd Ohio. The speed of the departing Confederates caused him to suspect that their hurry was caused by something more pressing than the Federals immediately in front of them. The thought stuck in his mind for 25 years.

When in Congress (1885-1889) Col. Jackson visited the Confederate Gen. Francis Marion Cockrell, a great uncle of mine, who was then a Senator from Missouri and asked him the direct question as to what drove them out of town, he replied, "Nothing drove us out. I watched the charge against your part of the line and when I saw you stay where you were I knew the town was no place for us and we got out of our own accord." See p. 83-84 of Jackson's diary. His company faced north on the right of Battery Robinette and lost two-thirds of its men in repulsing the Confederates at that point.

The Drives Against Robinette

The right wing of Gen. John C. Moore's brigade ran against Battery Robinette. I shall not go into close details. Three times in deep columns the Confederates formed, reformed and stormed that unfinished earthwork redoubt, and three times they were thrown back. The third time they carried the ditch, then completely filled with the dead and the dying, and also the outside of the work. The Federals were driven from their big guns—only the high earthwall separated the grim combatants—no man dared raise his head—it meant a brutal death.

Several reached the top of the earthen wall—they were killed and rolled backward down the embankment making a ghastly pile of dead men. The Federals were saved by the timely charge of troops rushing up from behind the redoubt and charging to the right and the left of the battery walls, and by shells from Battery Williams thrown into that mass of fighting men.

The pageantry of those Confederate charges is noticeable in the Federal reports.

It was here at Robinette that Col. W. P. Rogers of the 2nd Texas Infantry (J. C. Moore's Brigade) after forming his men outside of the woods in plan view, rode headlong to his death in the ditch in an effort to ride up and over the wall. His conspicuous bravery caused the Federals to bury his body upon the embankment. Today, an impressive monument to him stands alone in a block of ground on that ridge overlooking the town. It stands about fifty yards north of where stood Robinette and was unveiled August 15, 1912. There it stands —a solitary sentry of the gallantry and heroism of both the Blue and the Gray on that fall day when Corinth was saved for the Federals.

THE DRIVE AGAINST MCKEAN ON THE LEFT AT COLLEGE HILL

Here little fighting occurred. The Federals report only two attempts to approach Battery Phillips and claim heavy skirmishing. The Confederate Lovell did do some reconnoitering but hardly had that got under way when Villepigue was detached to support Maury's Division.

At another time that morning, Bowen, after feeling out his front with skirmishers, opened up with field artillery. He drew such a terrific cannonade that he knew that he had no chance of success so he retired behind a ridge and awaited orders. It was not long before the order for a full retreat came.

The Battle of Corinth was over—it was just twelve o'clock noon.

Inspector-General Cummings of the Confederates wrote, "Our lines melted under their fire like snow in thaw." But Federal Gen. James B. Weaver, who had little or no part in the deadly struggle, wrote in a lighter vein in his report. He said, "Oh! if there is upon this terrestrial sphere a boon, an offering which Heaven holds dear, 'tis the last libation liberty draws, from a heart that bleeds and dies in its cause."

The Confederates had been driven back into the woods. They had suffered severe losses, had run out of nearly everything, and were badly disorganized.

Again may I ask, where was Rosecrans' cavalry? Here was his perfect chance to throw in his idle cavalry and his unused troops—another chance to destroy that entire Confederate army, and he had all afternoon to do it.

After retiring into the woods, the Confederates showed in force in front of Robinette around one o'clock while gathering up the remnants of their battered forces. It was not until two o'clock that their retreat began. Burdened with their wounded, they strung out along the same narrow, dusty road and slowly moved, strangely alone and unmolested, some 10 miles back to Chewalla where they had bivouacked just two nights ago. Nothing disturbed the sleep of their weary troops—not even a single Federal cavalryman.

FEDERAL PURSUIT FROM CORINTH, A.M. OCT. 5TH

Orders for the pursuit were not issued until the evening of the 4th. Different columns were started in sundry directions. Various commanders aroused their tired men and started at all hours of the early morning of the 5th.

Stanley did not get away until the late hour of 8 a.m. It was a delayed start and a slow pursuit. Stanley, near Chewalla, took the wrong fork of the road, lost several hours, and then when he did find the right road, he ran into McKean's Division which was moving very slowly, encumbered by wagon trains—and this was a pursuit, mind you, of a defeated army.

Other commands of infantry had taken about every road that led westward. The whole shebang, parts of four divisions, came together on the same narrow road within a few miles. Hamilton's report complains about the resulting confusion and delay for want of a commander.

Many of the commands, starting before daylight, did not reach Chewalla 'till nightfall—a distance of only ten miles.

McPherson, in advance, did not strike the Confederate rear guard 'till he reached a hill, one mile south of Chewalla, that covered the main road. By that time it was noon. It was not until 4 p.m. and almost sunset when he caught up with the same rear guard at another hill at Young's house, some four miles further westward where the road goes down into the bottoms of the Tuscumbia.

McArthur, who had met McPherson on the same road, stopped for a long harangue with the Confederates under a flag of truce. Later he complained that he had lost three hours which gave Lovell's Division time to get away.

The Confederates out in front on the same road left it torn up aplenty. The Federal reports mention felled trees, abandoned wagons and artillery carriages left to block it. They were also lightening their carrying loads as they travelled—camp and garrison equipage, guns, artillery, ammunition and all sorts of stuff were strewn everywhere. Their trail was as plain as the noon-day sun.

By night of October 5th, Stanley and parts of other commands made camp about two miles east of the Tuscumbia. The Confederate rear guard had done a good job—they had held back the Federal advance to the short distance of about two miles for the afternoon.

Now LET'S LOOK at the Confederates. The main army or what was left of it had had a good night's rest—the first in a solid week, but food and water were dreadfully short, and the weather was hot. On the morning of the 5th, they lost no time and as they travelled, they left their severely wounded wherever they could find a house or old barn or shelter of any kind. They were headed for the same little old bridge over the Hatchie at the Davis house, then Metamora, where they would turn southward some twenty-eight miles to Ripley.

Their rear guard had shown that it could hold back the slow-moving Federals who had already frittered away precious advantages on the afternoon and night of the 4th and wasted the morning of the 5th. The main body of the Confederates certainly had nothing to fear from the Corinthian Federals who were trailing along behind them.

But they were concerned about what might be in front of them at the Davis bridge over the Hatchie. An energetic Federal force of fresh troops at the bridge could easily spell disaster.

You will remember that Wirt Adams had been left on the west bank of the Hatchie to guard the bridge, and that Hawkins' 1st Texas Legion had been left about two miles east of the Hatchie at Boneyard road to guard the wagon trains and to assist Adams upon call.

On the morning of the 5th, Adams with his 700 cavalry-men, were to the west of Metamora on the State Line road, and to the north on the Ripley-Pocahontas road to oppose any Federals coming from Bolivar, so Hawkins was ordered westward to guard the bridge. He was there early and in line of battle on the east side of the river.

For some unknown reason, Col. Adams ordered Hawkins to cross the bridge and advance toward Metamora at the top of the ridge and about a mile away. A little later, Gen. John C. Moore's brigade came up, or better his badly depleted brigade, and a number of his men crossed and advanced to Burr's branch, about 400 yards west of the Hatchie, where they connected with Hawkins' thin line.

By mid-morning of the 5th, the Confederates had perhaps 1,000 men across the bridge and on the west side of the Hatchie, and their main body, fairly well closed up, was approaching the bridge. A spiritless but overwhelming Federal force was slowly drawing nigh its rear from the east, and a fresh superior force of Federals was fast pressing in from the west against the Confederate front. Here the Federals had another chance to crush Van Dorn's entire army—again they threw it away.

Now let's turn to that force coming from the west—the Federal troops from Bolivar under Ord and Hurlbut.

FEDERAL ADVANCE FROM BOLIVAR A.M. OCT. 4TH

At daylight on October 4th, several hours before the crucial battle in Corinth began, the entire Federal command at Bolivar started on the Middleton road toward both Pocahontas and Metamora to gain the Davis bridge over the Hatchie. Some 8,000 fresh troops were in the line.

By nightfall they had travelled some 23 miles. The 1st Brigade under Lauman brushed aside the Confederate pickets between Middleton and the Big Muddy, crossed and camped for the night. The 2nd Brigade under Veatch camped on the west bank.

Late in the afternoon of the same day, the Federal cavalry drove the Confederate cavalry patrols under Wirt Adams back to Metamora, a small village on the ridge at the crossroads where they took refuge in and around the small buildings in the town under some protection from a piece or two of artillery that they had planted across the State Line road.

On the morning of the 5th, the Federal advance was retarded by the stout resistance of Wirt Adams and his cavalrymen, but Federal big guns soon routed him so he fell back to a hogback near Burr's branch where he found Hawkins' men and a part of the shrunken brigade of Gen. John C. Moore. Again, Federal artillery moved up and poured such a hot fire against the bridge that advancing Confederates could not cross.

During the morning, the Federals had travelled only about four miles and their infantry did not reach the bridge until somewhere between eleven and twelve-thirty o'clock. There was charge and counter-charge until a flank movement by a small body of Federals nearly gained the bridge behind the Confederates.

This sent the Confederates flying backward, and the Federals, flushed with success, made the same fatal error that the Confederates had made that morning. They crossed the Hatchie to attack, and their leading troops fell under murderous fire.

F EDERAL BIG GUNS that had been moved up played an important part, and again, masses of infantrymen unflinchingly started for the little bridge. The Confederates, now on the east side of the Hatchie, fell back further to the timber-clad heights where advance units of their main army had already arrived and had taken positions on a hilly ridge and on both sides of the State Line road.

In their headlong rush, the Federals crossed six regiments and then found themselves in a triangular pocket of low ground just about big enough for one regiment. Into that spot the Confederate artillery, slim as it was, poured a deadly fire.

Before the Federals could extricate themselves, they suffered severe losses in no time.

Federal artillery was crossed, the men spread out and stormed upward. Their superior force was not to be stopped. As Hurlbut wrote, "the field of Metamora had been won."

Some say the fight was over by 3:30 p.m. but others say it was about 5 p.m. Anyway, it was late on that October day.

After capturing the hill, the Federals stopped cold. In his report Hurlbut wrote, "The total want of sufficient transportation, the loss of battery horses, the shortness of provisions, and the paramount necessity of burying my dead, taking care of my wounded, and securing the prisoners and captured munitions of war prevented my pursuing."

In his congratulatory order he said, ". . . Already the victorious columns of Rosecrans were thundering on their (the Confederate) rear."

The Confederate rear-guard on the east side of the Tuscumbia bridge had left McPherson in no mood to get up too close, and now Hurlbut had had enough for the day.

While the Federals were being held back from the east and the west, the Confederate wagon trains at the Bone Yard road junction were unloosed and started south on the Bone Yard road and crossed the Hatchie at Crum's mill, some six miles up the river.

During the night, the Confederate army or what was left of it, countermarched about one and one-half miles to the same road and followed.

"The fight at the Hatchie was the last engagement," wrote Price. Van Dorn wrote that he was not molested on the retreat to Ripley, and on beyond westward to Holly Springs, although the enemy followed at a respectful distance. Cummings wrote that the enemy did not pursue with any great vigor.

Aᴠᴛᴇʀ ᴛʜᴇ ʙᴀᴛᴛʟᴇ at Corinth and the fight at the Hatchie, Grant seemed just as well satisfied as he and Halleck had been after Shiloh in April, the occupation of Corinth in May and the fight at Iuka in September.

But Rosecrans seemed to have grasped the value of pursuit, at least in theory, and was going it alone so far as Grant was concerned.

October 7th, from Jonesboro, he wired Grant not to call Hurlbut back. Later, at midnight, he wired, "Holly Springs will be ours when we want it—return will cause me to abandon chief fruits of victory—bend everything to push them while they are broken and hungry, weary and ill-supplied."

Later, at 2 a.m., from Crum's mill, he again wired Grant, "Out of rations—Hurlbut out of position and too much crippled to follow enemy—wants Sherman to set out for Holly Springs—wants men, food and a lot of other things—to push Confederates back to Mobile and Jackson (Miss.)."

October 8th, Grant wired Halleck in Washington that for the third time he had ordered Rosecrans to stop the pursuit. By that time, Rosecrans had reached Ripley. Halleck wired back to let Rosecrans go ahead and "live off the country."

Then Grant replied, ". . . although partial success might result from further pursuit, disaster would follow in the end. . . . Our troops would have suffered for food and already suffered greatly from fatigue."

That was Shiloh all over again except after that battle, it was Buell who was too tired from marching to undertake the pursuit.

Certain it is that Grant knew that the Confederates must be tired, too. Hadn't they marched something over a hundred miles in less than ten days, and spent three days of that time in furious fighting? Hadn't they been defeated with staggering losses, and now wasn't their shrunken army fleeing as fast as it could? That army lacked a heap of everything even when it started from Ripley—just read the testimony in Van Dorn's court martial.

Anyway, here we have a victorious Federal army being called back from Ripley under protection of fresh troops sent by Grant from Bolivar.

The significance of my comments become apparent when you look at the larger picture.

The end of June 1862 showed:

In the west: The Confederates had been driven out of Missouri, Northern Alabama, Kentucky, Middle and West Tennessee, Northern Mississippi and had lost every city on the river except Vicksburg. Obviously they had also lost the railroads in that vast area.

In the east: The Federal army stood at the gates of Richmond. Norfolk and the North Carolina sounds were gone. Savannah and Charleston were bottled up. Wilmington, North Carolina, alone was open to the Confederates and then only by running the blockade, so well remembered in W. W. Harney's "Blockade Running."

In the southeast: Pensacola was gone and Mobile was blockaded.

At Corinth, the Confederates tried a hazardous undertaking. Their savage attacks almost succeeded but they lost and paid dearly in men that they could not replace.

Between April and October they had been defeated three times, but Federal bungling, in turn, caused them to throw away their vast gains. They had failed to seize their advantages and fit them into the larger picture, thereby giving the Confederates a new lease of life that lasted two years—and all that time there was Robert E. Lee in Virginia.

It was not until the following July that Vicksburg fell. It could have been taken more easily after Corinth in May, or even after Corinth in October, 1862. That is a study for another day.

September 28th, at Ripley, the Confederates reported 22,000 men, but no figures were given for number of effectives, or number left there. At Corinth they had many less than 20,000, and their losses for the three days were reported at: Killed 505, wounded 2,150, missing 2,183—total 4,838.

At Corinth on the second day, the Federals had around 23,000, but no figures were given for the number of effectives. At the Hatchie, they had about 8,000 fresh additional men, consisting of twelve regiments of infantry, four batteries of light artillery, and three battalions of cavalry—all from Bolivar. Their losses for the three days were reported at: Killed 401, wounded 2,334, missing 355—total 3,090.

MONROE F. COCKRELL
1142 Hinman Avenue
Evanston, Illinois

INDEX

83

Van Dorn, Earl, Maj.Gen.; vi, 17-19, 21,
  22, 28-30, 34-36, 43, 45, 57-59, 61, 64,
  73, 75, 77
Van Dorn, Earl, Maj.Gen. (ill.); vii
VAN DORN, EARL, MAJ.GEN.,
  COURT-MARTIAL; 43-46
Van Dorn, Earl, Maj.Gen., Drinking
  Habits; 44
Veatch's Brigade; 36, 73
Vera Cruz, Mexico; 51
Vicksburg, MS; 57, 78
Villepigue's Brigade (J.B.); 23, 34, 48,
  61
Villepigue, John Bordenave, Brig.Gen.;
  69
Wade's Battery (Gates' Brig.); 47, 49
Ward, J.T., Col.; 46
Washington, TX; 51
Watson's Battery (Bowen's Brig.); 48
Weaver, James Baird, Brig.Gen.; 69, 70
West Tennessee; 57, 58, 61, 62
Wharton, TX; 51
Wharton, TX, Col. William P. Rogers
  Mon.; 6
White Handkerchief; 31
White House Line; 64
White House, Corinth, MS; 26, 27
White, --- (Armstead & White Studio);
  5
Whites of their Eyes; 39
Williams' Battery; 27, 66, 68
Wilmington, NC; 77
Wilson's Creek, MO; 18
Wisconsin Troops, Inf., 17th; 6
Wright, Uriel, Maj.; 43
Young House; 71
Young's Bridge; 21

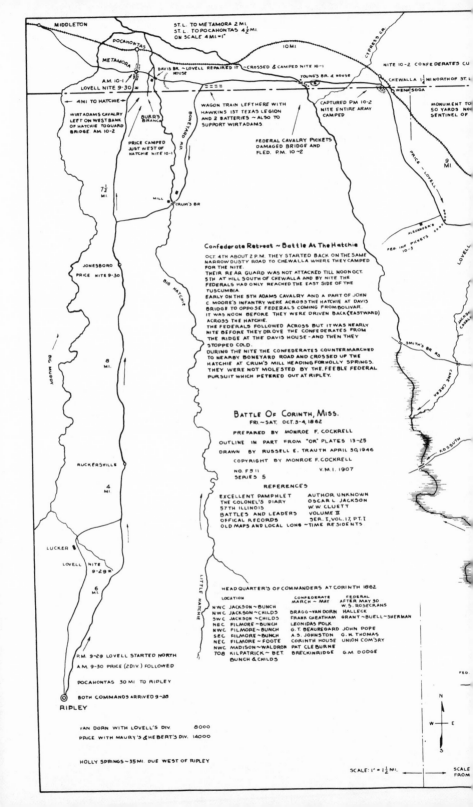

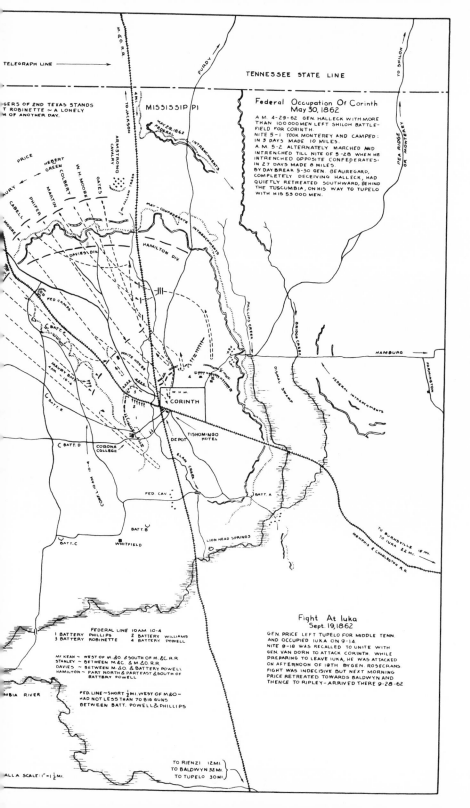

TELEGRAPH LINE ──────→

TENNESSEE STATE LINE

M & O R R

PURDY

TO SHILOH

MISSISSIPPI

GERS OF 2ND TEXAS STANDS
T ROBINETTE ~ A LONELY
M OF ANOTHER DAY.

MAY 28, 1862
FEDERAL

ARMSTRONG
CAVALRY

O JACKSON R R

INTRENCHMENTS

PEA RIDGE OR MONTEREY

Federal Occupation Of Corinth
May 30, 1862

A.M. 4-29-62 GEN. HALLECK WITH MORE
THAN 100 000 MEN LEFT SHILOH BATTLE-
FIELD FOR CORINTH.
NITE 5-1 TOOK MONTEREY AND CAMPED:
IN 3 DAYS MADE 10 MILES.
A.M. 5-2 ALTERNATELY MARCHED AND
INTRENCHED TILL NITE OF 5-28 WHEN HE
INTRENCHED OPPOSITE CONFEDERATES:
IN 27 DAYS MADE 8 MILES.
BY DAY BREAK 5-30 GEN. BEAUREGARD,
COMPLETELY DECEIVING HALLECK, HAD
QUIETLY RETREATED SOUTHWARD, BEHIND
THE TUSCUMBIA, ON HIS WAY TO TUPELO
WITH HIS 59 000 MEN.

PRICE
HEBERT GREEN COLBERT
MAURY
CABELL
PHIFER
MARTIN
MOORE
W. H. MOORE
GATES
DAVIES' DIV.
HAMILTON DIV.

MAY ─ CONFEDERATE INTRENCHMENTS

PHILLIPS CREEK

BRIDGE CREEK

FED CAMPS

BATT. E

HAMBURG ──────→

WHITE HOUSE

MAURY B. M

BATT. E

CORINTH
W.H.M.

FEDERAL INTRENCHMENTS

FARMINGTON

ELAM CREEK

BATT. D

CORONA COLLEGE

DEPOT

TISHOMINGO HOTEL

ELAM CREEK

FED. CAV.

BATT. A

TO BURNSVILLE
TO IUKA 22 MI.

MEMPHIS & CHARLESTON R R

BATT. B

LION HEAD SPRINGS

BATT. C

WHITFIELD

Fight At Iuka
Sept. 19, 1862

GEN. PRICE LEFT TUPELO FOR MIDDLE TENN.
AND OCCUPIED IUKA ON 9-14.
NITE 9-18 WAS RECALLED TO UNITE WITH
GEN. VAN DORN TO ATTACK CORINTH. WHILE
PREPARING TO LEAVE IUKA, HE WAS ATTACKED
ON AFTERNOON OF 19TH BY GEN. ROSECRANS.
FIGHT WAS INDECISIVE BUT NEXT MORNING
PRICE RETREATED TOWARDS BALDWYN AND
THENCE TO RIPLEY - ARRIVED THERE 9-28-62

FEDERAL LINE 10AM 10-4
1 BATTERY PHILLIPS   2 BATTERY WILLIAMS
3 BATTERY ROBINETTE   4 BATTERY POWELL

MC KEAN ~ WEST OF M.&O. & SOUTH OF M.&C. R.R.
STANLEY ~ BETWEEN M.&C. & M.&O. R.R.
DAVIES ~ BETWEEN M.&O. & BATTERY POWELL
HAMILTON ~ PART NORTH & PART EAST & SOUTH OF
            BATTERY POWELL

BIA RIVER

FED. LINE ~ SHORT ½ MI. WEST OF M&O ~
HAD NOT LESS THAN 70 BIG GUNS
BETWEEN BATT. POWELL & PHILLIPS

ALL A SCALE: 1" = 1½ MI.

TO RIENZI 12 MI.
TO BALDWYN 32 MI.
TO TUPELO 30 MI.